ARGUE LESS LOVE MORE

PRAISE FOR
'ARGUE LESS – LOVE MORE'.

"Get the book and study it. Understanding and avoiding the 5 hurtful mistakes Paul points out in this book will help you prevent many of your upsets and arguments and bring back open and honest communication to your relationship."

— Scott Catamas - Love Coach Academy

"We felt we could tackle our issues, learn practical communication skills, and get mastery of them faster and more directly than we had in two years of traditional couples counseling.

–G.S. Denver, Colorado

"It opened up our communications beautifully…"

— Dr. L.C. Boulder, Colorado

"I came to Paul as a last ditch effort to save my relationship. I had tried everything I could think of to get my relationship "unstuck" over many years and nothing worked.

I came to Paul as a last ditch effort to save my relationship. I had tried everything I could think of to get my relationship "required advanced attack/defense routines that would play-out over-and-over without resolution.

I truly appreciate Paul's ability to get right to the heart of the issues that my wife and I had been experiencing for many years. Having tried marriage counseling (unsuccessfully) earlier in our relationship, we were both a bit skeptical about trying a coach. We figured if a psychologist couldn't help, then how could a relationship coach be of benefit.

All I can say is, that I'm glad we took the chance with Paul - it's making a huge difference for us. As a couple, we interact differently and have largely ridded ourselves of the detrimental communication patterns we had fallen into and couldn't get out of by ourselves. We are happier and more open with one another now and enjoy the new space that has opened up for us."

– M.C. San Diego, California

"We are so grateful to Paul for working his magic on us! We have been married for 25 years and still could not figure out how to communicate effectively to each other without blowing things all out of proportion and feelings getting hurt.

Paul gave us some simple tools to use the very first session and we noticed a difference right away. Each week we learned more tools and Paul helped us to strengthen the ones he taught us in the beginning.

Our relationship had never been better, our only regret is we did not find him 25 years ago."

– R & S Phoenix, Arizona

"We were an hour and a half into our drive home when I realized we were talking about our toughest issues with calm compassion and understanding instead of upset and hurt. Thank you so much for such an amazing gift."

– C. S. Estes Park, Colorado

"It was a journey of intimacy with myself and others. Thank you for sharing this transformational communication tool!"

– A.J. Golden, Colorado

"I now feel like I have the security in my thoughts to convey myself for a brighter future with my mate…"

"I felt so lost and full of despair about my new relationship... I didn't feel like any of my words were getting through. I couldn't convey myself in a healthy manner; this class showed me I had options to turn despair into hope. I now feel like I have the security in my thoughts to convey myself for a brighter future with my mate."

– L.T. Denver, Colorado

"The techniques allowed me to feel empowered. I am able to envision endless opportunities to apply these techniques for my own relationships, for my job, and in the community at large when confronted with difficult situations or even to help focus on problem or needs of others."

– L.N. Elkins, Arkansas

ARGUE LESS
LOVE MORE

5 Communication Secrets
For Couples Who Want
Less Pain And More Passion

PAUL STERLING

Argue Less – Love More
©2016 Paul Sterling

ISBN: 978-0-9980834-2-1

Magic Relationship Method
www.MagicRelationship.com

Printed in the United States of America

DEDICATION

To the amazing women that have loved and educated me in the ways of relationships. I am forever grateful…

and to my many powerful and wise mentors for sharing their wisdom—Bob Proctor, Marshall Thurber, Tony Robbins, Richard Bandler, Robert Kiyosaki, Byron Katie, and Marshall Rosenberg.

Paul Sterling
Argue Less – Love More

Limits of Liability/Disclaimer of Warranty:

TABLE OF CONTENTS

Introduction. 1

Destructive Habit 1: Case-Building 17

Destructive Habit 2: Storytelling 35

Destructive Habit 3: Message-Assuming. 49

Destructive Habit 4: Cup-Stuffing 69

Destructive Habit 5: The Fatal F's 83

Make Extraordinary Communication A Reality 101

Book Summary 111

About The Author 119

INTRODUCTION

> "The quality of your relationship is based on the quality of your communication. Change the way you communicate and it will change your relationship."

By picking up this book, you've decided that you want more from your relationship. Specifically, you know that there are better ways to have open, honest, and intimate communication. You're in luck! You are well on your way to having more of what you want. This book will help you identify and, more importantly, avoid some common communication mistakes and show you how to build constructive habits in their places.

At the beginning of a relationship, everything is blissful. You talk for hours getting to know the most intimate details about each other. You can discuss anything and your partner is receptive and understanding. This is the person you want to spend your life with, share with, and love. Can you remember how utterly amazing this feels?

But then, something happens and little things start to go wrong.

The next thing you know, small upsets become big issues and misunderstandings blow up into arguments. Even basic daily communication becomes more and more difficult. It feels impossible to choose a brand of toilet paper or a place to eat on a Friday night without a massive fight erupting; you start to feel defeated.

Without the right communication tools and skills, even your best efforts seem to make things worse. Pretty soon, you and your partner are walking around on eggshells and you both start to avoid communicating.

Communicating feels fruitless and frustrating, so why even try? You start to feel hopeless.

The closeness you once had erodes away every time you avoid a conversation with your partner. Soon the chasm is so vast that you don't even know if you are in a relationship anymore.

I know how it feels when this happens, when you want so badly to make it work and you just can't seem to find the right words.

There is a better way to relate. This book can help. The MRM (Magic Relationship Method) provides some simple, straightforward, step-by-step strategies that can make love, intimacy, and compassion, easier.

How to use this book:

1. **Print.** This book is full of interactive exercises. I know everything is electronic these days, but printing this out will allow you to fully interact with the text. So dig some blank paper out of the bottom of your closet, refill that ink cartridge, and hit the print button.

2. **Read. Take turns reading this** book out loud to each other and do the exercises together. Use the time to connect and relate with each other. Put your computing devices away and give it your full attention. It might sound scary: just you, your partner, and a stack of paper, but trust me, it'll be worth it.

3. **Play. Make it fun, and do it as a team.** Remember that doing this with your partner brings you both closer. Together, you are both discovering more effective ways to communicate so you can feel how much you love each other. When you get upset, it is so easy to view your partner as the enemy. These communication tools are designed to help you turn that around!

4. **Breathe.** When you start to feel reactive, take deep breaths. They give you a moment to think and deliver more oxygen to your brain. Sometimes, if you take a moment to breathe deeply, you'll decide that the spatula in your hand is better for flipping eggs than it is for throwing at your partner's head. Breathing is especially helpful when dealing with confronting material that gets covered in the exercises in this book. So,

try it now. See how good it feels to have an oxygenated brain!

5. **Laugh.** This is so important! When communication breaks down and we start to feel the other person slipping away, everything seems like life or death; it all feels *very* serious. It helps to take a step back and look at how we all make mistakes, and sometimes, they are funny. Did you really think that the way your partner squirted the toothpaste from the container was an indication that he or she didn't love you? Did your partner's face turn bright red because you forgot to hang up a wet towel? Not taking yourself or your habits too seriously is the first step towards change.

Why am I so passionate about compassionate communication?

There are times when you try and communicate with your partner about something emotional, like being jealous, but end up yelling about his or her inability to empty the dishwasher instead. Talking about the real important and emotional issues like money, trust, respect, and sex, intimately, openly, and honestly is hard, but it is a critical relationship skill that is built with practice.

The question is: how can we practice doing something that we were never taught to do?

Have you ever felt that trying to communicate with your partner is like trying to build Ikea furniture where the pieces are supposed to come together and create something, but you have no idea how, or in what order without the instruction manual? And maybe, if you just shove this one piece hard enough, it'll fit.

I definitely needed an instruction manual.

Like most people, I learned how to communicate—and how to with-hold communication--from my parents. They did the best they could with the tools they had, but were unable to make their marriage work. Their weak communication tools cracked under pressure.

I communicated with my ex-wife the best way I knew how. I struggled with creating softness and closeness between us. I mostly told her what to do, when to do it, and then asked her to report back to me when she was done. As you can imagine, this did not inspire intimacy.

One divorce and three broken engagements later, I started wondering if I would ever get it right, or if I were destined to screw up every important relationship in my life. I had no idea what was going on. I had met some incredible women, and I just wasn't sure why every relationship kept falling apart.

So, I was intrigued when my best friend, who was having major challenges in his marriage, said he was learning a new way to communicate from Dr. Marshall Rosenberg. I thought my friend's relationship was dead in the water, but Dr. Rosenberg's communication tools brought it back to life from the edge of divorce.

I had to know more. Learning these communication secrets became my quest, Dr. Marshall Rosenberg (now deceased) became my mentor, and, finally, helping other couples became my life's work.

Marshall's system is called "Nonviolent Communication" (NVC). (You can find out more about his work at www.cnvc.org) I studied and taught this method of relationship communication for eleven years. I blended my understanding of Dr. Rosenberg's nonviolent communication principles with Neuro-Linguistic Programming (NLP), Neuro-Associative Conditioning, and Systems Theory, to create an incredibly effective way to compassionately connect with others.

I had to throw out the old tools like shame, blame, guilt, anger and manipulation and learn how to replace them. I found a whole new set of tools such as compassionate communication, empathy, and intimacy. Now, I have created an instruction manual to go with tools.

What I discovered was a better way of communicating.

When relating (or fighting tooth and nail) with my partner, at some point, I noticed a pattern:

When the intensity of my emotions increased, my intelligence decreased.

Think about what happens when you fight: objects are thrown or kicked. You scream things that you would never say to your partner under normal circumstances when you are in your right mind. The more emotional you get, the less logical you become.

All of the sudden, you have lost control, and it doesn't matter what the other person says. You become that kid in the grocery store, laid out and pounding fists on the tile floor, demanding the sugary cereal, completely unwilling to listen to logic or to be consoled.

In moments when emotions flare and rationality are thrown out the window, you need a communication toolbox - or even better - before things get out of control.

Magic Relationship Method (MRM)

The Magic Relationship Method is that better way; and this is the manual you've been looking for.

This method will help you transform misunderstandings, arguments, and breakdowns in your relationship, into compassion, understanding, honesty, and open communication. It gives you a simple and compassionate way to discuss the most difficult issues with your lover.

Take a deep breath. You don't have to struggle anymore.

The Magic Relationship Method is a distillation of my life experiences as well as many years of learning from my mentors, coaches, teachers, and advisers.

I've spent over twenty years studying with some of the best communicators: Tony Robbins, Richard Bandler, Robert Kiyosaki, Bob Proctor, Marshall Thurber, Byron Katie and Marshall Rosenberg; and I've combined, condensed, and simplified what I've learned from these communication masters into The Magic Relationship Method.

I've taught and tested this method with thousands of people in some of the toughest places I know. I've brought it to maximum-security prison inmates, at-risk teenage students, and high-school teachers. I've taught university professors, therapists, and couples' counselors to use this method with their clients as well as in their own relationships.

And, of course, I've taught hundreds of couples.

MRM has worked in all of these situations and it can work for you too. It consists of three phases:

Phase 1. Stop Doing Damage.

Stop the 5 destructive habits and replace them with the 5 healthy habits.

The first phase (covered by this book) will teach you how to recognize and overcome the five relationship-wrecking communication habits. Eliminating these nasty habits will make an instant, noticeable improvement in the quality of your relationship.

Phase 2. Bridge the Gap between the Two of You.

The 4-Step Intimacy Formula

In this phase (covered in the next e-Book) you will discover how to rebuild intimacy, trust, and understanding. You will experience a sense of confidence and compassion as you increase your ability to have open, honest, and loving communication with your partner and connect more deeply.

Phase 3. Create a Bright Future

The 7-Relationship Rules.

These simple relationship rules, covered in the third book, will help you clarify and understand what it takes to keep love alive. You will learn to make agreements that build trust, honesty, and intimacy, in order to create the future you want with your partner.

Time to Meet the Enemy: The Five Destructive Habits

You're about to discover the destructive communication habits that can wreck your loving relationship. I teach this first so you can stop these habits before they do any more damage.

You will also learn how to replace them with positive helpful habits. Start today and make a difference in the *quality of your relationship* right now.

When you become aware of your habits, you will be able to talk about important, emotional topics without making them personal. You will actually be able to communicate about almost anything without throwing insults, using coercion, or wrecking your relationship.

You will learn how to feel less shame, blame, guilt, duty, and obligation, all of which can have detrimental effects on your relationship. You will have the tools to stop avoiding communication with your partner and start looking forward to talking about important issues.

Overcoming the five destructive habits and replacing them with five effective habits gives a strong foundation for a thriving relationship filled with happiness, harmony, compassion, and understanding.

You will discover how to talk and have your partner actually *want* to listen. You will discover how to listen so your partner will want to speak freely and honestly with you.

It also works in other types of situations – in the boardroom, kitchen, at work, and at school, it even works in jails. You name it and it's been tested there.

In addition, the MRM has helped parents reconcile with grown children who they have not spoken to for years, and it has helped open up communication between siblings who decided to stop talking to each other because of past misunderstandings.

And, of course, these tools have saved many couples from going through the painful heartbreak of divorce or separation.

All of these people suffered because they didn't have the communication skills and tools they needed.

Most relationships are destroyed because of a lack of skills, not because of a lack of love.

This book is your precious guide to more intimacy, heartfelt connection, and compassionate understanding in all of your relationships. Read it again and again. Highlight it, underline key points, make footnotes, and most importantly, do the exercises.

Then, **practice, practice, practice.**

Let this book launch you on a journey to a heart-opening flow of great communication, intimacy, and love.

Creating the Right Mindset for Relationship Success

> **To create the relationship of your dreams, you don't need a different partner. You just need to know how to communicate with the one you already have in a different way.**

Some of what I'm about to share with you will seem counter-intuitive, unusual, and uncomfortable. I invite you to see communication in a totally new light. Your willingness to get out of your comfort zone is going to be key to your success.

There are so many times when we think we need to work harder, but, in fact, all we need is a shift in perspective.

For example, one day on the ski slopes, I was making my way down an expert run when I saw a man walking up the hill with only one ski. I asked if I could help him find the other one, but he politely declined any assistance.

He was sure that he didn't need any help. He was sure that he was headed in the right direction, and he was sure that if he worked a little harder and trudged a little farther, he would achieve his goal.

Because I absolutely could not resist being helpful, I yelled up to the people on the chair lift who were right above us and asked if they had seen his ski. Sure enough, from their improved vantage point, they could see the missing ski, and pointed to it about thirty feet *downhill* from where we stood. He was working really hard, but headed in the wrong direction.

This happens with couples all of the time.

They work really hard, certain they are headed in the right direction. They refuse to get help because they are embarrassed, proud, and are so sure that if they work a little harder, they really won't need help after all. I know, I've been there, struggling up the hill earnestly looking for that darn ski.

But sometimes, all it takes is talking to someone who has some perspective who can turn us around instantly and head us in a more helpful and effective direction.

The purpose of this method is to give you that improved perspective like the people had from the chair lift. When you gain enough perspective, you can move your relationship in a helpful, productive, and positive direction, and you can reduce the amount of stress, conflict, upsets, drama, and misunderstandings.

Change

> **"Change isn't always better... but better is always change!" Marshall Thurber**

Recognizing your habits is the first step toward changing them. If you don't notice the fact that you are biting your nails, how can you stop doing it? Often, my friend gets nervous at a horror movie or a meeting, looks at her hands, and realizes she has bitten off all her nails. She doesn't even remember doing it.

First, she has to become aware every time she raises her finger to her teeth. Once she is aware, she can see a moment when she has a choice. If she notices that her nails are two inches from her teeth, in that moment, she can choose to chomp down on her nails or back away from her fingers and put her hand down.

The way we communicate is based on a series of similar choices. Sometimes, your first choice happens so fast that you may not even be aware that you made a decision. If you make a choice often enough, it can become unconscious and it becomes a habit.

If you slow things down and then back up far enough, you can start to recognize habits as choices again. Only then, can you begin to change them if you want to.

It's important to realize when you're making changes in your relationship, even positive ones, that you will run into some resistance. When you change, you build new emotional muscles and, at first, it can be challenging.

For example, when you go to the gym after not working out for a long time, your whole body aches after only 10 minutes on the exercise bike. But then, in a couple of weeks, you can climb that stair master like it's nothing for an hour straight because you have built up muscle and endurance. At first, things will probably be uncomfortable, that just means you're getting a good work out.

HABIT 1: CASE-BUILDING

Case-Building

When you are communicating with someone over an emotional issue, you need to ask yourself is:

"Do I want to build a connection with them or a case against them?"

Building a connection creates compassion, trust, and intimacy.

It leaves both parties feeling loved, appreciated, and understood.

Building a case creates defensiveness, resistance, and resentment, and leaves them feeling bad, stupid, and wrong (BSW).

"I'm Right. You're Wrong. Anything you say can, and will, be used against you."

This decision can happen so fast that you may not even be aware that you made a choice, but you did. **The choice you make is going to decide what type of relationship you create.**

Building a case is when someone gathers evidence and uses it to prove a point. Usually, the point the Case-Builder is trying to make is that he or she is right and that you are wrong, in which case, you should be very sorry and do whatever your partner tells you to do. Most people end up retreating from Case-Builders into the safety of silence. The Case-Builder normally wants to be understood without understanding the other person's perspective.

This form of communication is not about avoiding issues. There are times when your partner does something that needs to be talked about. How much better off would we be if we could just talk about it without talking about who is right or who is wrong or whose fault it is?

It's a common trap to think that if you show your lover how right you are and how wrong s/he is that your partner will be overwhelmed with your logical evidence. Then, your partner will surely see your wisdom, have a change of heart, and say thank you for setting them straight.

The problem is when you build a case against your partner, it actually drives them farther away and decreases intimacy.

What you really want to do is build intimacy instead. No one wants to make their partner feel like a failure. But, case-building does that and can show up in tiny little ways; it will bleed your relationship dry like a million paper cuts.

Slow down and listen to yourself. The following words are warning indicators that you might be building a case:

- should/shouldn't

- have to/must/can't

- right/wrong

- good/bad/evil

- always/every/never

What your partner hears is that s/he is bad, stupid, or wrong, and needs to change.

You can build your case with the best of intentions and from love. You might even be *right*, but, it doesn't matter if you're right. Case-Building comes from the assumption that if we build a strong enough case against our partner the behavior will change.

Not going to happen!

Have you ever tried to convince:

- a smoker to quit?

- an alcoholic to stop drinking?

- an out of shape person to work out?

- your kids to stop fighting?

- a jealous lover to not be jealous?

- an overweight person to eat less?

- an addict to give up drugs?

You get the idea.

Case-Building doesn't help your case. Our judgments prevent us from getting the message across. We can try and manipulate someone into doing what we want, and sometimes, we might even get our partner to capitulate in the short term; but a person has to want to change in order to *really* change. When we build a case, we don't respect the other person's autonomy and intelligence.

We are saying that we know how *they* should live their lives better than they do.

So, when you feel yourself getting riled up, and you start flipping through that mental Rolodex of everything your partner has done wrong, pause, and recognize that this habit is rearing its' head. Then, you can decide if you want to create more intimacy or push your partner a little farther away.

You are building a case if . . .

- you use listening to gather evidence to prove you're right and s/he is wrong.

- you try to express your point louder or more forcefully than your partner.

- you try to convince your partner that you have been wronged.

- you're using your lover's history to try to make him or her feel bad, stupid, and wrong.

- you think you are right and that you aren't interested in understanding them.

To build a connection.

> ## "Seek first to understand,
> ## then to be understood."
> ## Stephen R Covey

Instead of building a case, learn to speak and listen courageously and compassionately. Build a connection of intimacy, honesty, openness, and trust, with your lover.

Discover how to relate to your partner. To step into their shoes and into their world, the first thing you need to do is listen to him or her so s/he feels heard, understood, and valued.

While listening, look for what your partner is feeling, needing, and requesting. It's a real gift when you do that for your partner.

Note: This form of communication will also work with your kids, your parents, or anyone you care for.

When emotions are high and issues are important, it will be tempting to build your case. When your partner does that, it makes your whole body cringe. So instead of reacting, take a deep breath and remember that breaking a bad habit takes willpower and strength. Exercising your connection-building muscle means working it out on a regular basis, even when you don't want to.

You are building a connection if . . .

- you say, "Tell me more..." and you mean it!

- you ask for clarification or feedback

- you listen twice as much as you talk.

- your lover opens up, is vulnerable with you, and trusts you enough to talk about his or her feelings, needs, dreams, desires, fears, and frustrations.

- you want your partner to feel understood before asking him or her to understand you.

Examples:
Here are some examples of **Case-Building** versus **Connection-Building**:

You haven't made love in over a month. You think something is wrong, and you are afraid of asking for what you want because you don't want to be rejected again.

The Case-Building Approach:

"We haven't had sex in months! If you were eating right and exercising, your sex drive would be higher and you would want me. You should join the gym and stop eating junk food. Aren't you committed to our relationship? Your sister started working out and doing yoga, and she said her sex life with her husband has never been better. I was really patient a couple of weeks ago, but I've waited months and you still don't have any interest. How do you think this makes me feel?"

When you say these things, your lover typically feels attacked and responds defensively. There isn't much room for discussion around the actual issue. If this conversation results in lovemaking at all, it will be out of a sense of duty and obligation, not love and connection. And usually, that type of lovemaking is *not* very fun. But luckily, there's another option!

Choosing to create a connection, and to be open and vulnerable about your need for physical intimacy, is much more enticing to your partner; it will bring your partner closer to you and turn him or her back into a lover.

The Connection-Building Approach:

"I've noticed that we haven't had sex in over a month. I really miss that level of physical intimacy with you. I have a story going on in my head that it is because you don't find me attractive any more. Is that true or is there something else? What desires do you have? Would you be willing to tell me what comes up for you when you think about making love again?"

After asking these questions, really listen to the answer and try to enter your partner's world. Repeat back what you think you heard so it's understood that you are both on the same page.

When you build a connection, you take an emotional risk and you're vulnerable; you talk about the real issue at hand. When you Case-Build, you just talk about why your partner is bad, stupid, and wrong, for not giving you what you want.

I don't recommend starting with your most difficult, emotionally charged issues. When you're learning how to ski, you start on the bunny slope, and once you've learned the basics, then you move to the more difficult terrain. It's the same thing here.

If you start with easier issues (like taking out the garbage or making the bed), instead of more difficult issues, (like why your husband hates your mother, or how you feel about your partner's spending habits), you give yourself a better chance of success.

Here's an example of using this tool with a family member:

Your teenage daughter comes home from school and tells you that she wants to go to a party Friday night. She says that there won't be any parents there, but not to worry because this boy is a totally cool guy and *über* responsible. She's wondering if maybe she could spend the night too. A bunch of her friends will be staying, and she just wants to save you from the hassle of picking her up really late. She reminds you that she'll have her cell phone so it's really no big deal.

You might feel your fists clench and heat rise in your face. You are about to launch into a rendition of, *"When I was your age, I would never...,"* or maybe, with similarly effective, *"How dare you even ask,"* or, possibly, *"What is wrong with you that you would even consider..."*

In this moment, before you say anything, you have a choice. You can build a case against her (based on logic and maybe even experience) or you can connect with her.

Case-Building: *There's no way in hell you are going to that party. I know kids today with their drugs and alcohol. I've seen the ten-o'clock news. And I don't care how "über responsible" this boy is. I know what teenage boys want. No way. You're NOT going! End of story.*

The case-building approach is very tempting because it makes you feel strong and in control for a while, but consider the long-term impact on your relationship.

Not good.

So, how can you build a connection instead?

If you want to be understood by others, start by understanding them. Then, ask them to understand you.

If you don't understand, care about, or respect the other person's feelings and needs, then how can you expect them to understand, care about, or respect yours? For this to really work, they have to understand that you understand them. They have to feel that you are entering their world. Lip service is not enough.

Building Connection*: **In the example above, here's what the mother could ask her daughter:** "When you think of spending time at the party with your friends on Friday night, do you feel excited because your needs for fun and acceptance will be met?"

Then, listen to what she says. Keep repeating what she says back to her until she feels **heard**, **understood**, and **valued**. It may seem like a slow way to communicate, but because you are taking the time to deal with the underlying issues, they get resolved rather than recycled again, and again, and again.

Your daughter will be amazed that somebody could possibly understand her feelings and needs... especially you!

Once she feels heard and understood, there is a much better chance that she will hear your concerns and needs: she'll understand that you are frightened, that you have a need for her safety and well-being , and that letting her go to the party will not meet your needs.

Once you've established the feelings and needs on both sides of the conversation, then the two of you can discuss ways in which both of you can get your needs met.

In the end, you might say, "No". But saying " No", after you have taken the time to understand and show respect to your daughter, will build a connection with her. If you can get the point across that you don't know how to get your needs and her needs met at the same time, she will be more likely to respect your decision.

SUMMARY

Old Destructive Habit:

Building a Case.

The old habit is where you gather evidence to use against your partner. One obvious clue that you are building a case is if you try to prove that you are good, smart, and right by making the other person bad, stupid, or wrong. Or, if you are using guilt, blame, and shame to manipulate your love, then it is clear that you care more about wanting to be understood than about wanting to understand them.

When you build a case, you think you know what your partner should or shouldn't be doing. Once you realize that that is what you are doing, you can re-choose to build a connection instead.

New Productive Habit:

Building a Connection. You choose very quickly to either build a case against your partner or build a connection with him or her. If you start building a case, remember to slow down, take a deep breath, and build a connection. Focus on listening with empathy and compassion first. Make sure you understand first, and then try to be understood by sharing your feelings and needs openly and honestly.

Practice

Exercise #1. The next time you're watching TV or a movie, watch for examples of Case-Building. Jot them down on the following page, share notes, and talk to your partner when it's over.

Watch, listen, and learn! It's always easier when you're watching someone else do the case-building. Make it a contest to see who can identify the most case-building in a single TV show or movie.

Great shows that exhibit case-building are: Law and Order, Modern Family, The Big Bang Theory, NCIS and the list goes on.

Program: _____

Character: _____

Words used: _____

Evidence gathered: _____

How they made someone BSW (Bad, Stupid, & Wrong):

_____

Exercise #2. Next, turn up the emotional thermostat! Examine some of your conversations and look for **Case-Building** at work, with relatives, or neighbors. Share your discoveries with your lover.

Person: _____

Situation: _____

Words used: _____

Evidence gathered: _____

How they (or you) made someone BSW: (Bad, Stupid & Wrong):

_____

Exercise #3. Keep the mercury rising! Remember a time when you built a case against your partner. Write it down and share the information.

Situation: _____

Words used: _____

Evidence gathered: _____

How you are making them BSW_(Bad, Stupid, & Wrong):

_____

ADVANCED-TRAINING-VIDEO PRESENTATIONS

As a special bonus gift to you for purchasing this book, I am giving you free access to my 7-part advanced relationship-communication series.

In this first video, we will explore why the people you love the most can be the most difficult to talk to, and what to do about it.

Video #1
THE RELATIONSHIP-WRECKING CYCLE

In this video, I cover:

1. Compassionate communication tools for couples. It's like having a relationship toolbox to help you resolve conflicts, clear up misunderstandings, and talk about important/tough issues without taking things personally and making them personal.

2. The hidden power your past relationships have over your current love life… Is your history wrecking your future?

3. What controls whether or not,your relationship will become a loving and compassionate success or a heartbreaking and painful failure - you gotta know this!

4. What's the one thing you need to change if you want your relationship to change. Most couples never understand this and it can cost them their relationship!

o to www.MagicRelationship.net/bookbonus.htm ,enter you name and email dress, and get instant access to your free videos today.

HABIT 2: STORYTELLING

> **"I have been through some terrible things in my life, some of which actually happened."**
> **Mark Twain**

Creating Stories

"That's my story and I'm sticking to it."

Every day we have countless experiences: we see people on the street; we talk to coworkers; we interact with family; we chat with friends; and we connect with our partner. Your mind works hard to make sense of all of this input. To do that, you create stories.

Because the mind was designed to keep us safe, it tends to be protective, and it often overreacts; it can't tell the difference between danger and discomfort and will often confuse simple, harmless comments with attacks from your partner. When it does, it tells us a scary story and we react defensively or even attack back. When we believe these stories, we get stuck in them.

Example: "Oh no, *she's looking at me in that way again. What did I do wrong now"*

She can tell him that there's nothing wrong and that she was just looking at him. But if he tells himself the story with enough emotion, conviction, and repetition, he will start to believe that the story is true. There will be nothing she can say or do to convince him otherwise.

Example: "*I can't believe he didn't hug me when I came in the door today. What is wrong with him? The love in our relationship must be dwindling."*

Maybe he's tired from work or maybe he's hungry and focused on thinking about what he'll have for dinner. But if she believes that he didn't hug her because he is angry or because the relationship is falling apart, it will be very difficult for him to convince her that anything else is true. If he tries to talk to her about it, she might even say that he can't *really* just be tired; there **must** be something else wrong.

When your mind tells you a story about **why** somebody did something, recognize that it is just a story and make sure to check it out before believing it.

You know you are stuck in your story if . . .

- you're unwilling to hear your partner's side of things.

- you're sure that you're right, and they're wrong, and that's that.

- you're embarrassed and afraid to tell your partner what's going on in your head.

- your reaction is totally out of proportion to what is actually happening.

- you're try to get all your friends to agree that you're right and your partner is wrong.

- You believe that there is only one way to see things and it's your way.

Here's a story that a past lover made up about me:

"Each night, when Paul was done reading, he turned off the bedroom overhead light leaving me reading by my bedside lamp, alone. After a while, it really hurt my feelings and ended up pissing me off!

Why should he have a great light for reading while I had to make do with a little lamp"

"The story I told myself was that he didn't care about me. My needs weren't important to him.

Finally, one night, I decided I couldn't take this anymore and had to say something about this to Paul. I told him my story and what it meant to me when he turned off the overhead light while I was still reading.

To my surprise, he listened; he didn't try to defend himself, and he repeated back what I told him so I knew he got it. He totally understood how I could feel the way I did because of the story I was telling myself. Once I was done, he asked if I'd be willing to hear his story.

Here is Paul's version: since the light switch was on his side of the bed, he thought he was helping me by turning out the light. He was saving me the trouble of having to get out of bed!

The next night when Paul went to turn out the light, he stopped; he remembered our conversation and asked me if I wanted him to leave the light on?

My response, because of my new story was, "No way! I don't want to have to get up and turn it off! But, thanks for asking!"

What a difference understanding each other's stories made!"

Story-Busting

The first step is realizing that you told yourself a story. Then, next is sharing your story openly and honestly. This technique will help you keep your relationship open, honest, and intimate. It's also a great way to clear up misunderstandings.

Share your story before you start believing it. If you wait and let it fester and grow inside your head, you will start ***building a case*** based on that story. These destructive communication habits build on each other.

Example of Storytelling AND Case-Building:

*"He's so quiet and withdrawn today, he must not care about me. Now that I think about it, he's been withdrawn for weeks. He **never** pays any attention to me anymore. If he were a good husband, he would give me more love and affection."*

Checking out your story is simple, but not always easy. It can make you feel uncomfortable, embarrassed, and vulnerable. Your story exposes your fears, doubts, and weaknesses.

In the example above, her story showed that she secretly wasn't feeling loved and that it wasn't okay for her to ask for her needs to be met. That is a tough truth.

Example of checking out a story: *"I'm telling myself that you're withdrawn because you are angry with me or you don't care about me. What's going on? Is this true? Are we okay?"*

When checking out a story include the words, **'I'm telling myself a story'** in your question, and end with, **'Is this true?'** This may seem weirdly artificial at first, but it helps the other person hear what you are saying without trying to defend themselves.

Without it, the question sounds more like an accusation: *"You came home late three nights in a row, and you just don't care about me any more! Do you?"*

With it, the question creates an opening: *"When you came home late from work three nights in a row. I told myself a story that you don't care about me any more. What's going on? Is this true?"*

(The last example was based on a story about a couple who are my friends. It turns out that when he confronted his wife about the whole situation, she was working overtime so she could buy him a computer as a birthday present. Surprise!)

Using the word 'story' also helps create an opening in both people's minds that another valid point of view exists.

Facing that truth together creates intimacy. Letting your partner see and feel your insecurities is what being in an intimate, vulnerable, and honest relationship is all about. It can bring your relationship to a whole new level.

You are checking out stories if . . .

- your partner is upset, and you say, "I wonder what story you are telling yourself?"

- you tell your story, and then you ask, "Is it true?" After discovering that a painful story you believed wasn't true, you hug your partner, say thank you, and both have a good laugh.

- you listen and understand your partner's responses.

- you stop yourself when using words like "You always", "You never "or "You're wrong".

- you see that your partner has a story and instead of getting defensive, you ask about it.

Storytelling in Action

Example: One day a man walked into a law office and said he wanted his lawyer to handle his divorce. The lawyer asked, "*Why do you want to get divorced?*" Here's his story: the other night he'd gone to pick up his wife after her shift at work, and when he got there she was sitting in another man's car, talking.

Well, it was clear to the husband that something was going on and that meant the marriage was over. There was nothing to talk about,, no opening for her point of view. He was **stuck in his story** and that was that.

The attorney continued to ask questions partly out of legal necessity and partly out of curiosity.

On the night in question, there was a snowstorm; it was late and cold. She was waiting in a dark deserted parking lot and the other man happened to be the wife's boss. He offered to stay with her until her husband arrived to protect her from the storm.

But, that's not the story the husband told himself.

In his mind, she no longer loved him. She had betrayed him and his trust.

When you don't check your story with your partner, you experience your story as reality; it becomes "The Truth".

Here's another example: Your partner and you normally make love once or twice a week. Several weeks go by with no sex and your partner is still not interested.

Stuck in Your Story:

"You never want to make love any more. You're becoming cold, frigid, and distant. You must not find me attractive anymore! Are you sleeping with someone else?"

When you communicate from the place of being stuck in your story, your lover feels attacked, gets defensive, and then, often, attacks back.

Checking out your Story:

"It's been several weeks since we made love. I'm feeling scared and a little hurt and I'm telling myself the story that you don't find me attractive any more. What's going on for you? Is that true?"

Notice how this is really addressing the issue, not dodging or avoiding it. You're dealing with it head-on, but in a healthy way.

You've just created the possibility for open, honest, vulnerable, and compassionate communication. Talking this way will feel a little awkward, uncomfortable, and unfamiliar at first. You're building the muscle. Stay with it; communicating this way gets easier.

SUMMARY

Old Destructive Habit: Storytelling.

Someone gets stuck in their story and tries to "convince" themselves-and everyone else- that they are right.

Your mind makes up stories about your situation in an attempt to protect you and keep you safe. You get stuck in the story when you believe it is true even though you have not checked it out with your partner. When you are stuck in your story, you will say things like, "You always", "You never", or "You're wrong". You have a strong feeling that you are absolutely right, they are wrong, and there is only one way to see things: *your* way; that is the only way it could be.

New Productive Habit: Story-Busting

You realize that your mind is doing its job by making up stories to try and keep you safe, so you examine your stories. You say to your partner, "I am telling myself a story that ..." and when you are done, ask him or her, "Is it true?" If things feel off between you two, look at what story you are telling yourself, and then ask your partner to do the same. Check out your story first, and then help your partner to check out their story. End of story!

EXERCISES

Exercise #1. Share Stories

First, think of some stories you were told when you were younger that you totally believed at the time and found out later that they weren't true. What about Santa Claus? The Easter Bunny? The Tooth Fairy? And, babies come from storks?

Write down one of these stories from your past, and then share it with your partner. Be sure to include any behaviors that demonstrated the conviction of your beliefs.

_____

_____

_____

_____

_____

_____

_____

Exercise #2 Turn the volume up!

Write out one example from your relationship where you or your lover believed a story and acted on it, but it wasn't true. What was the story? How did you feel about it? This can be a story you told about your partner or one he or she told about you. Then, share it with your partner!

Example: *"When my husband showed up late from work three days in a row, I made him sleep on the couch because I was convinced he was cheating on me. In fact, he just had to communicate with some clients in Asia."*

_____

_____

_____

_____

_____

_____

_____

Exercise #3 Now, really crank it!

Write a story that you are currently telling yourself about your relationship.

Example: "I'm telling myself the story that if I tell you I'm scared about applying for a new job that you'll lose respect for me. Is that true?"

"I'm *telling myself the story that* _____

_____ "

_____ . *Is that true?*"

ADVANCED-TRAINING-VIDEO PRESENTATIONS

Ready to dive deeper? There are seven video presentations waiting for you on advanced-relationship-communication skills.

In the second video, we will explore one of the most important relationship skill of all. Most people don't know what it is… but it's CRITICAL for keeping your relationship together.

Video #2
RELATIONSHIP PROBLEMS… RESOLVED OR JUST RECYCLED?

In this video, I cover:

1. The secrets that cause some relationships to spiral upwards into happily ever after while others spiral down into heartbreaking divorce…

2. Why most relationship problems painfully recycle over and over again rather than lovingly resolve once and for all.

3. How to change one simple sentence in the way you describe your problem that will totally transform the results you get in your relationship. It takes you from being a victim in your relationship to being in control.

Go to www.MagicRelationship.net/bookbonus.htm, enter you name and email address, and get instant access to your free videos today.

HABIT 3: MESSAGE-ASSUMING

When Mind Reading Goes Bad

Message Said versus Message Heard

This is where it is often assumed that when you communicate, you simply say what you mean; the other person hears the message (what you said) and gets that message exactly as you intended. But, communication is rarely that simple.

In fact, communication can be pretty complicated. We all have experienced a wide variety of situations in our lives. Every time someone talks to us, we listen to the words and filter those words through our own experiences. For example, when I hear the word, "home", I think of the house I grew up in. I picture the high ceilings, cool tile floors, and spiral staircase. A house is a place flooded with sunlight and full of the wild animals that we adopted as pets.

We say words with a certain intention and intonation. The words and tone then mingle with the experiences of the person we are talking to and together they create the meaning.

For example: The question, "Honey, can you take out the trash?" can mean a variety of things.

"If you love me, you'll take out the trash."

Or, *"My father always took out the trash, which means it is the man's job so get to it, buster!"*

Or, *"You sat home all day watching TV and you didn't smell that? Can you get your lazy ass off the couch for five seconds and take care of this?"*

Or, *"If you loved me, you would have already taken out the trash. Your lack of motivation is proof that you don't love me any more!"*

Or, **"***I am an awful person because I am asking you to take out the trash instead of doing it myself. Will you still love me anyway?"*

Or, **"***I'm running late, or I'd do it myself. Please be a dear and take out the trash. I appreciate and love you!"*

When we are listening, how do we know what our lover is *actually* saying? When we are speaking, how do we know that's what our lover is actually hearing?

Often, we assume that our partner got the right message, the message we intended. We think that what we said was so clear and so undisputable that there is no way it could be misunderstood. "*I really appreciate that he's taking out the trash, but why is he scowling at me? I didn't think it was that big of a deal.*"

Or, we assume that we understood what was said. We think the exact message we heard was the message our partner intended. "*Why is she getting on my case for being lazy again? I didn't even know the trash needed to be taken out!*"

People have a tendency to hear the message filtered through the story going on inside their heads instead of listening to the actual words being spoken. Usually, we don't take the time to clarify; we assume our interpretation matches the speaker's intentions.

Leaping to Conclusions

The next form of "Message-Assuming" shows up when you leap to a conclusion and stop *listening.* This normally happens because you think you know what is going to be said.

Here is an example from my life when I was "Message-Assuming".

One day, my friend Dave called and asked if I'd like to go white-water kayaking with him. I love kayaking. It's one of my obsessions. So, I said, "Yes" without any hesitation.

Dave told me to meet him at the bridge, and then continued to share more details. We normally meet at the Dairy Queen Bridge, so I assumed that's what Dave meant so I stopped listening.

Not only did I stop listening, but my mind also drifted. And while Dave kept talking, I went over the details of what needed to be done before I could leave. I started to think about what gear I would need. I told Dave I would see him later and hung up the phone.

I showed up at the Dairy Queen Bridge, but Dave wasn't there. A half-hour later, Dave still wasn't there. What was going on?

How could he do this? What kind of a friend has me rush to meet him, and then just doesn't show? I cursed loudly and thought about what a jerk and a bad friend he was. I started blaming, even vilifying, him.

The problem wasn't Dave. He *actually* said that he was going to Mary's Lake Bridge that day, not the Dairy Queen Bridge. So while I was waiting for him, he was actually waiting for me at Mary's Lake Bridge. He was equally annoyed, seething at a different bridge.

This whole fiasco is a classic case of the destructive habit of Message-Assuming.

As soon as I thought I knew what Dave was going to say, I stopped paying attention. I was excited to go kayaking.

Adrenaline and emotions can interfere with our ability to stay present and hear what is actually being said.

You know you are Message-Assuming when . . .

- you interrupt someone because you think you know what is going to be said next.

- you end up at a different restaurant than your partner and you blame him/her.

- you stop listening before your lover is done talking and start preparing what you want to say next.

- you respond to only the first part of your partner's message.

- you share something that is very important and do not ask what was heard.

Message-Clarifying

What could I have done differently to avoid the misunderstanding with Dave? It's as simple as ordering pizza. Think about the last time that you called out for pizza. The person who took your order knew that it could be easily misunderstand as to what you were saying. So, what did they do to overcome this obstacle and solve this problem? **They repeated what they thought they heard.**

It goes like this: *"Thank you, Mr. Jones, for your order. Let me repeat it back to you to make sure I got it right. That was a 16-inch pepperoni pizza, to be delivered to 2123 Smith Ave. Your phone number is (415) 555-1212 and your credit card number is 1234-5678-91011. Is that right?"*

All I needed to do with Dave was repeat back the gist of what I thought I heard. *"Dave, do you want to meet at the Dairy Queen Bridge at 1:45? Did I get it right?"*

Dave would have caught the misunderstanding before it became a problem. This is a simple, powerful, and effective tool. But, it isn't normal communication.

Ordering pizza isn't a very emotional event. It becomes more important to take steps to avoid Message-Assuming when emotions are running high like they do in many of your intimate relationship communications.

- **Remember, when emotions increase, intelligence decreases.** The more important and emotional the message the more important it is to make sure the ***message sent*** is actually the ***message received***. If you are doing the talking and want to make sure that you are heard and understood, you can make the clarifying request: *"Would you mind telling me what you heard me say?"*

  On the other hand, if you are listening and want to make sure that you received the intended message, you can ask, *"Can I tell you what I heard you say?"* Or, you can say, *"I heard you say ____. Is this right?"* This simple method is effective and profound. The person speaking feels heard, understood, and valued.

Message-Clarifying Guidelines

1. **40-Word Maximum:** If what you're talking about is really important or emotional, go slowly and take it in small chunks. If your partner gets confused or lost, you'll know exactly where you lost him or her in the conversation and you'll be able to get things right back on track. Never go more than 40 words without checking in with the other person to make sure that the message you're sending is the message being received.

2. Ask, *"Would you tell me what you heard me say?"* Or... if they are talking, you stop them at about 40 words and say, *"Can I stop you for a second and catch up? I want to make sure I'm following you. Let me tell you what I think I heard you say..."* In a normal conversation, you may go a lot longer than 40 words, but when you are talking about your relationship and other emotional stuff, it's good to have conversations go slowly and in small chunks. Checking in often makes sure the conversation stays on track.

3. **When you are going to talk about something emotional or important, tell your partner,** don't ambush them! Start by saying, *"This is important and I want to make sure that I*

explain it clearly so that I'm understood." Also, tell them, *"I know there are times when I think I'm being clear and I'm really not, so from time to time I may ask you tell me what you think you heard me say. Okay?"*

It's good to practice on small issues where there's not too much at stake and emotions aren't running high.

If your partner is resistant to this practice, it's likely that s/he is thinking, *"You think I don't know how to listen and I'm stupid."* Explain that you are trying to be responsible for your communication, and that, sometimes, what you want to say and what someone else hears are different.

Also, let your partner know that you're committed to under-standing what s/he has to say. To do that, you would like to practice telling your partner what you think you heard, espe-cially when the communication is important or emotional.

4. When people tell you what they thought they heard, no mat-ter how different from what you thought you said, **Always THANK them and never CORRECT them.** Take responsi-bility for sharing your message in a way your partner can hear it. Keep communicating until both the message said and the message received are the same. Don't blame your partner for not hearing what you are saying.

People mistakenly believe that the more they talk the better chance they have of being understood. NOT SO! In fact, it's the opposite.

The truth is, the more words they use and the more talking they do, the greater the chance of confusion and misunderstandings unless they keep things on track by using the **message-clarifying habit.**

You are Message-Clarifying if . . .

- your lover is done talking and you say, *"Let me tell you what I think I heard you say...."*

- at the end of your statement, you ask the listener, *"Could you tell me what you*

- *heard me say?"*

- when you don't understand, you say, *"Tell me more"* or *"I don't understand; can you tell me in a different way?"*

- you use short sentences, give feedback, and make message-clarifying requests when what you're talking about is important and emotionally charged.

Example. I was working with a couple at one of my Argue Less, Love More Seminars where I teach compassionate communication to couples. This couple told me about a misunderstanding they were having. The woman, Donna, was very upset with her partner, Joe. He kept moving her personal things, including her make-up, to different places around the bathroom.

Each morning when she was getting ready for work, she had to hunt down what she needed. One time, he put her hair dryer in a drawer and rearranged the medicine cabinet. He shoved her eye shadow to the back of the shelf and moved her lipstick and eyeliner into a different drawer in order to make room for his shampoo and deodorant.

Using the skills she learned from the MRM, Donna told Joe: *"I have a need to have integrity at work, which means showing up right at nine. When you move my things, I have to spend time looking for them in the morning, which interferes with this need. I feel frustrated and hurt, and I would like some support here. Would you be willing to tell me what you heard me say?"*

"Yeah," Joe responded, *You said, "I'm an asshole for touching your things."* As you can see here, the message he heard was very different than the message she sent. He didn't hear her message; he only heard what was going on inside his own head.

Donna responded calmly by saying, *"Thank you."* She didn't correct him. This is an important factor. After all, Joe had done what she had asked; he told her what he heard. Donna stayed committed to her communication and responsible for the outcome. Rather than blaming him for not hearing her correctly, she just asked if it would be okay if she tried again.

He nodded, "Yes."

So, Donna continued in a compassionate tone, *"I feel frustrated and hurt because I have a need for simplicity and ease when getting ready for work. Would you tell me what you heard me say?"* (Don't underestimate the power of your body language and your tone of voice!)

"Yeah," he threw back at her, "You *want me to stop touching your things."* Once again, he may have been caught in his own fears and been unable to hear her message.

"Thank you," replied Donna, and then she tried again, and again, and again, AND AGAIN! How many times do you do it? Until it is done!

It took eight rounds of Donna expressing her feelings and needs before Joe could reflect back accurately the message she was sharing with him.

We all cheered when he said, *"You're frustrated and hurt because you have a need for simplicity, ease, and support in the morning."*

If right now, you're saying, "Damn, that's a lot of work!" The truth is, yes, it can take some time and focus, but it's not nearly as much work or as painful as the destruction of a relationship because of misunderstandings.

In normal communication between couples, they have no way of noticing exactly when the conversation went off-track and Message-Assuming took over.

SUMMARY

Old Destructive Habit:

Message-Assuming.

When speaking, you share a message and jump to the conclusion that the person listening to you heard the message you intended him or her to hear. When listening, you assume that you understand what your partner is saying without telling him or her what you think you heard. Sometimes, you even think you know what your partner is going to say and you stop listening before they are done talking.

New Productive Habit: Message-Clarifying.

You recognize that the message sent is rarely the message received. You use clarifying sentences such as, *"Can you tell me what you heard me say?"* when you are the speaker and *"Can I tell you what I heard you say?"* when you are listening.

Practice Exercise #1. Notice Message-Assuming

First, practice noticing the habit of Message-Assuming. A simple and less confrontational way to do this is by watching sitcoms. These shows are full of Message-Assuming. You can watch them together and laugh with your partner as you both learn. Make some notes, and compare them after each show.

Words used: _____

_____

_____

Message assumed by listener: _____

_____

_____

Message intended by speaker: _____

_____

_____

Exercise #2. Practice Message-Clarifying

Next, practice using message-clarifying sentences. Follow these steps:

When You Are Speaking:

1. You want to make sure that you're understood. One way to do that is to end with the sentence, "Can you tell me what you heard me say?"

2. Make sure to thank your partner no matter how different his or her answer is from what you intended to say.

3. Repeat until you feel heard, understood, and valued.

When You Are listening:

1. Listen and feeback what you think you heard. To make sure you understand, use the sentence, "Can I tell you what I think I heard?"

2. Use the 40-words-maximum rule. Make sure to stop before hitting 40 words and check if the message being sent is the message being received.

3. Repeat until they feel heard, understood and valued.

Practice this at least once a day.

Exercise #3. Listen to your partner

Listen to your partner and notice when there's an implied or incomplete message that ends without a clear request. Practice asking message-clarifying questions on interactions that are not emotionally charged so you can get the hang of it.

Example: Your partner asks, 'Are you going to the kitchen?'

Instead of guessing what they might want, you reply, "Is there something in the kitchen that you would like me to get you?"

"Oh no", your partner replies. "I just want to see if the dishwasher is done yet; could you check?"

By asking the message-clarifying question, you are able to **uncover the underlying and unspoken message or request.**

When you communicate this way, remember it's not about getting it right. It's about engaging in a process and a type of communication that leads to clarity and understanding.

Exercise #4. Watch for Message-Assuming

Watch for Message-Assuming and use the space below to write down your discoveries; what was said and what was the message assumed:

_____

_____

_____

_____

Now, discover what was really meant: the clarified message:

_____

_____

_____

_____

_____

Exercise #5. Give instructions

This process works in any relationships. When you give directions, instructions, make plans, or express something personal about your-self., try asking others, *"Would you be willing to tell me what you heard me say?"*

Notice when people get what you intended to say and notice when they don't. Again, don't attempt to make your partner feel bad for any misunderstanding. Just say, "Thank you", and clarify. The more you do this exercise, the more you'll realize just how common the message-assuming habit is.

Note discrepancies here: message sent vs. message received

_____

_____

_____

_____

_____

When somebody is making plans with you, giving you directions, instructions, or revealing deep, personal information, ask them, *"Can I tell you what I think I heard you say?"*

First, you'll be amazed at how many misunderstandings and upsets this will avoid.

Secondly, you'll be amazed at how much more compassion, understanding and intimacy you'll achieve checking in like this builds when you're talking about emotional issues.

Message Sent vs. Message You Received.

_____

_____

_____

_____

_____

ADVANCED-TRAINING-VIDEO PRESENTATIONS

The Beatles were wrong! Love isn't all you need… Discover what destroys even the most loving relationships, if it's not addressed. Seven advanced-relationship- video presentations are waiting for you. In the third video, we will explore why love isn't all you need.

Video #3
WHEN LOVE ISN'T ENOUGH… ARE YOUR PROBLEMS BIGGER THAN YOUR SKILLS?

In this video, I cover:

1. Specific skills you need to stop your relationship from falling apart Most crumble because they lack these skills, not due to a lack of love.

2. How to stop avoiding the important emotional issues that need to be talked about rather than having to hide from them and walking around on the eggshells.

3. The most important choice you can make when communicating with your lover – this one alone can be a relationship saver!

Go to www.MagicRelationship.net/bookbonus.htm, enter your name and email address, and get instant access to your free videos today.

HABIT 4: CUP-STUFFING

> "When you listen with empathy to another person, you give that person psychological air."
> – Stephen R. Covey

Cup-Stuffing is the straw that broke the relationship's back.

Mary sits in the car for about thirty seconds after pulling into the garage, then she walks into the house and starts to think about the interesting day she had at work. She can't wait to tell her husband, Rick, all about it.

But as she walks in the door of her home, the incessant beeping of the smoke alarm instantly jars her.

When she gets to the kitchen, she sees Rick standing on a chair in the middle of the smoke-filled kitchen trying to dismantle the alarm. The veggies on the stove are burning and their youngest daughter is crying. As she takes her daughter into her arms, she starts to tell Rick about her workday. Mary begins to talk to him about her great presentation and how well she did. She thinks she might get a bonus. She asks, " Isn't that exciting?"

Rather than answering, he stares down at her from his perch, his face tight and red, and the fighting begins. Does this sound familiar?

When you try to get someone to listen to you or do something for you when they are already emotionally or physically over-whelmed, you are *Cup-Stuffing*. The person's emotional cup is already full and you trying to fit more in.

It can happen at any time. Yet, it happens most when you and your partner come back together after being apart, typically when returning home from the workday. With all the challenges and stresses of the day, it can be hard to hear anything your partner has to say even if it's good news! It may feel like he or she is trying to stuff something into your already full cup, causing you to overflow, erupt, or have a total meltdown.

It's even worse when two full cups collide!

This is not limited to you and your partner; it is the same with any-one you talk to. If someone's cup is full of upsets, emotions, and problems, the person can't hear you. Or, if your cup is full, you can't hear what others have to say.

It's not a matter of choice, it's a matter of physics. It's not personal. It's not that your lover doesn't want to listen to you; it's that he or she is full. It's like when you can no longer store any more data on your hard drive because it has no memory left. Something has to be deleted before something new can be saved.

Your Cup Is Already Stuffed When . . .

- you try listening to your partner and can't hear a single word he or she is saying because you are too overwhelmed. you tell your partner that you just can't handle one more thing, you run into your bedroom and slam the door when you are asked for a glass of water.

- your kids ask if they can watch TV and you start screaming I can't take this anymore!" and threaten a severe punishment.

You Are Cup-Stuffing When . . .

- your partner is already stressed out and you try to have an important conversation without checking in first.

- you see your partner after a day apart and you automatically start sharing your upsets and frustrations without asking if they can hear you now.

- you try to talk to your partner when he or she is very focused on something else (for example: watching television, having a phone conversation, working on the computer, or driving in a snowstorm).

- your partner asks for a break and you don't stop talking.

Recognizing and avoiding Cup-Stuffing can bring great relief to both of you. The first step to stopping this habit is for you to become aware that you are doing it. Then, you can shift gears and help your partner empty his or her cup. This is referred to as Cup-Emptying.

When **people's cups are too full**, they normally need a **healthy dose of empathy** to unwind, decompress, and let go of tension. Your willingness to tune into your partner's experience and give him or her a hand at key moments goes a long way toward creating connection.

For example, years ago, I was living with someone who taught *at-risk* high-school students. She was stuck between her students, resistant angry teens, and the over-controlling administration.

By the end of the day, she would come home with a very full cup.

My days were full of coaching couples from around the world. I would help them resolve their relationship problems by transforming the way they communicated, which is what I do to this day. I also write, design, and deliver e-Books and articles, and arrange workshops. A lot of the time, both of our emotional cups were very full by the time we came back together at the end of the day. To avoid big fights with hurt feelings, we used the Cup-Full Rule: we told each other when our cups were full, and then agreed to come back later and connect.

Instead of insisting that your needs get met right away, give your partner space to breathe and perhaps step in to help.

After a short break, many times the process of connecting and giving empathy can go much more smoothly.

When you listen and empathize with your partner, they can move from being overwhelmed with challenging emotions to being present and available to hear you.

If both partners have full cups, then take turns sharing a little at a time giving and receiving support and empathy along the way. Maybe take a short break first. Use the 40-Word-Max Rule. At moments when both of you are on tilt, short exchanges can help you listen to each other without feeling overwhelmed by the exchange.

Here are some tips to help you go from Cup-Stuffing to Cup-Emptying.

Tip #1. Set up a 'Warning Cup-Full' Agreement.

Discuss Cup-Stuffing with your partner. Come to an agreement that when either of you has a full cup or can't listen that you'll let the other know by saying, "*CUP FULL!*, or "*I'm overwhelmed; let's come back and talk in a half an hour.*"

Tip #2. **If you want to be heard, check-in in advance, Ask,** *"Is now is a good time?"* **before diving into difficult topics.**

If you are the listener, let your partner know if you can hear them now … or not.

Example: *"I was thinking about our conversation from last night and I was wondering if you have a few minutes so I can share my thoughts and feelings with you."* When your partner agrees, you share. If not, an agreement is made about a different time that the two of you can discuss the issue.

Tip #3. **If you try to talk to your lover, and he or she says , "Cup full", you can ask him or her, "Do you want empathy or do you want space?"**

If your lover chooses empathy, you can engage in emptying his or her cup by listening, empathizing, and then feeding back a condensed version of what you just heard. If your lover chooses space, you can wait, come together later, and talk about whatever needs to be discussed at that time.

Tip #4. **Empty your own cup**

After a long day of teaching communication skills to prison inmates, my cup was really full! So, I would do something special for myself before going home; this would empty my cup. In the summertime, my favorite thing to do is spend a couple of hours white-water kay-aking. Afterwards, I feel energized and able to give attention to my partner.

What works for you? It could be exercising, walking, reading, writing, talking to a good friend, having a cup of tea, rubbing your partner's feet, or having him or her rub yours. Try and find a variety of ways to decompress.

Remember, "Cup full" or "I Am overwhelmed" isn't personal; it only means that your partner can't hear you right now, not that you've been cut off. This is much better for the relationship than having your lover pretend to be listening when he or she is not capable of it at that time.

If you've told your partner that your cup is full, be responsible. You made an agreement, so make sure you follow-up later and listen to them. If you don't, he or she may assume that when you say, 'Cup full', it really means that you are blowing them off. It will erode the trust and limit your ability to use this communication tool.

One of the most common questions I get when coaching a couple is *"How do I provide empathy?"* This subject is covered in more detail in my next book, but here are some quick guidelines:

- When giving empathy, you are not trying to fix your part-ner or provide solutions. Just listen with the intent to hear, understand, and enter their world.

- If you're receiving empathy and you're talking about your relationship, remember to focus on the facts of what happened and how you feel about it. It's best not to make judgments about your partner or slip into the blame, shame, guilt game.

- Stay in physical contact with your partner during the process if possible.

Let's go back to Mary and Rick at the beginning of this chapter. What would that kitchen scene have looked like if both parties had been practicing **Cup-Emptying?**

Instead of heading straight home, Mary could have stopped at her favorite bookstore and browsed the shelves for about half an hour. She could have picked out a novel and then headed back home. Next, she would have gotten out of the car eager to share her workday with Rick, but feeling calm and light.

In that case, Mary might have said, " *Hi Rick. It looks like you might be overwhelmed right now. I had a crazy day at work and would love to tell you about it, but can I help you out a little bit first? What can I do?*"

Then, Rick might have replied, "*That would be great! Thanks! I totally ruined the broccoli. Could you sauté some more so we can get dinner done. I've had an insane day too, and I'm looking forward to getting the cooking out of the way so we can connect. I definitely want to hear about your work when we get settled and start eating.*"

Mary: "*That sounds great, I can't wait to tell you about it.*"

You're Cup-Emptying When . . .

your partner comes home stressed out and you greet him or her with the question, *"Do you want empathy for your hard day or space to decompress?"*

you offer to listen without giving ideas or advice.

after empathizing with your partner you ask, *"Is there anything else you need?"* before you start sharing your own stuff (day?).

You say, *"Cup Full"* to your partner, then you take a break, and connect later when you are ready to listen.

SUMMARY

Old Destructive Habit:

Cup-Stuffing

When we share with people who aren't able to hear us, because they are full of thoughts and emotions. Their emotional cup is full, and if we don't take the time to see that they are overwhelmed they may explode, melt down, or just tune you out; the same is true if your cup is full.

New Productive Habit: Cup Emptying

Notice when your cup is full or when your partner's cup is full.

Give your lover empathy by listening compassionately and by giving them a chance to express their problems, burdens, and anything else that they find overwhelming.

Give some space to the other person or take some space for yourself when needed- before trying to connect again. You have certain things you do to help you decompress, like go for a run, hike in the mountains, read a good book, or jump in a lake. When you come back together, you focus on listening and giving compassionate support or receiving compassion from your partner.

Practice

Exercise #1.

When was the last time that somebody tried talking to you when your cup was full? How did it feel? How much do you remember? What did you do? What did you say?

_____

_____

_____

_____

What would you do differently now that you know about this destructive Cup-Stuffing habit?

_____

_____

_____

_____

_____

Exercise #2.

Practice asking these key questions:

"Do you want empathy or do you want space?"

"I'd like to talk to you about _____ .
Is now a good time?"

"My cup is full right now. Can I get back to you in _____
minutes?"

How did these questions change your interactions with your partner?

_____

_____

_____

_____

_____

ADVANCED-TRAINING-VIDEO PRESENTATIONS

In the fourth video, "Can You Hear Me Now?", I will uncover what people really want when they are talking. This is REALLY IMPORTANT. I will also show you the (obvious once you know it) counterintuitive solution to most communication problems.

Video #4
CAN YOU HEAR ME NOW?
The 2 Parts Of Communication

In this video, I cover:

1. The little-known, but very powerful, secret to keeping open, honest, and loving communication going in your relationship.

2. What to never say to your partner!

3. That counterintuitive (but obvious, you know, it) solution to most communication problems.

4. What is the language of lovers that will increase the amount of compassion, understanding and support you experience on a daily basis.

pend less time in reaction and more in harmony and partnership.

nderstand what your lover really wants when they are talking to you.

s a special gift to you I am giving you free access to my 7-part advanced relationship-communication series.

o to www.MagicRelationship.net/bookbonus.htm and enter you name and ail and get instant access to your free videos today.

HABIT 5: THE FATAL F'S

"Let me tell you what to do and how to do it"

Fixing, Fighting, and Fleeing

Your partner comes to you after work. S/he sighs heavily. You can tell s/he's upset. S/he takes a deep breath and says, *"Hey, I'm having some trouble at work, do you have time to talk? I could really use some support."* (It's off to a good start. S/he's making sure that your cup isn't too full.)

You reply, *"Thanks for checking in honey. I have time, let's talk. What's up?"*

S/he says, *"I just can't take it anymore. I am totally stressed out and overworked. My stupid boss, once again, changed my job description to include more duties without additional pay. I already have to bring work home just to keep up as it is."*

What do you do? The person you love is hurting. S/he's trapped in a painful situation and doesn't seem to know how to get out of it.

You see exactly what your partner *should do* to fix the problem, and as soon as s/he stops talking, you swoop in to the rescue, offering your brilliant advice, hoping for respect, appreciation, and maybe even some affection.

First, you try and *FIX* things!

In a calm voice, you say, *"Honey, here's what you're going to do: just say no. Tell your boss politely, but firmly, you are not going to do it. She should hire some extra help or at least give you a raise. You're totally capable of standing up to her; I know you are!"*

To your surprise, rather than being appreciative, thankful, or even mildly interested in receiving your wisdom and advice, your partner becomes even more upset turning the full force of his or her anger, pain, and frustration, on you.

It's our natural inclination to offer our wisdom and ideas to the people we care about. But, the problem is that they feel we are trying to "FIX" them. At work, we are rewarded for fixing things. We are valued and paid for the problems we can solve and the good advice we give.

At home, giving advice (especially when it's unrequested advice) or trying to problem solve can have the opposite effect. Rather than helping, this behavior can destroy trust, intimacy, and understanding. It also inhibits open and honest communication. Go figure.

You persist because, after all, your partner has to do something. When you continue, his or her response is to lash out at you and say, *"You have no idea what is really going on at work! Do you think I'm stupid? Do you think I haven't thought of that? It's not that simple."*

When you try to fix someone, the message you send is that they don't know what they should do, and you do.

Most of the time, when people are venting frustrations, they simply want to know that someone is listening and cares. They want to know that they are heard, understood, and valued.

When your partner blows up at you for giving advice, it's confusing. And now, you're angry with him or her for being temperamental and defensive. You were just trying to help. You were being supportive, listening, and offering a perfectly good solution. Weren't you doing the right thing?

You may even say, *"I didn't say anything about you being stupid. I just didn't want your boss taking advantage of you. I wanted to help you stand up for yourself."* Instead of having the calming effect you were hoping for, your partner is now totally pissed off and you're now in the FIGHTING phase.

Out of desperation, you try and stop the discussion from completely falling apart with a comment like, *"Honey, let's calm down and get some dinner, and we can talk about what you can say to your boss tomorrow."*

Your partner says, *"You just don't get it! I'm going to go have dinner with my friend who understands problems like this."*

Finally, when fighting becomes too much, someone flees.

After all, why stick around once you've fought over the same issue for the hundredth time? You already know the outcome.

Next thing you know, your partner is headed out the door to go hang out at the bar with his or her ex-college roommate while you sit at home, eating warmed-up leftovers and wondering what the hell went wrong.

Fleeing can happen in several different ways:

Physically: by leaving the scene.

Emotionally: by attacking back, or shutting down and disconnecting from your partner.

Verbally: by retreating into the silent treatment and avoiding the topic altogether.

This destructive habit is very common. Be compassionate with your-self and your partner as you become aware of these habits and start to replace them. When you see yourself trying to fix your partner or your partner trying to fix you and you're getting frustrated, stop and take a breath. Take a moment to remember your commitment to creating intimacy and great communication with your lover.

You are Fixing, Fighting or Fleeing if . . .

- you jump in with advice, suggestions, and/or solutions to your partner's problem before s/he is even done talking.

- you feel like you need to rescue your partner because they will screw it up if you don't help.

- you leave the room in the middle of a conversation because you get too emotional or frustrated.

- you say, "I don't want to talk about it any more!"

- your partner's eyes roll, s/he sighs loudly, or otherwise communicates disinterest in another one of your good ideas.

- you tell your partner, "I don't know why the hell I bother telling you anything because you never do what I say."

The good news is that there is a simple and effective solution. With only one key question and a few sentences, you can prevent the Fatal F's from escalating or even appearing. With practice, you can stop this habit in its tracks long before it gets out of hand.

Empathetic Listening: Always Offer EMPATHY FIRST!

Once you make the decision to stop fixing people and start listening to them with compassion, acceptance, and understanding, they will love you for it.

The next time someone comes to you hurt, angry, upset, scared, or overwhelmed by something, stop and ask this simple, relationship-saving question:

"Do you want empathy or advice?"

It will take the conversation in a totally different direction. When you offer options, your lover will opt for empathy before advice most of the time.

People crave the opportunity to be heard and understood without any advice, criticism, or judgment.

Empathetic listening is so rare that it's a true gift. It is a simple, powerful, and loving habit to develop.

Once you make the decision to stop fixing people and to start listening to them with empathy, compassion, and understanding, you will radically increase the trust, honesty, and open communication.

It will take practice. Fixing is a hard habit to overcome, and you may have to bite your tongue more than once.

Let's look at the same scenario from earlier in the chapter, but this time using empathetic listening instead of jumping in and trying to fix the situation.

Your partner tells you about his or her problem at work. Instead of trying to fix it you say, *"Honey that sounds like a tough situation and you sound pretty stressed out about it. I'm wondering if you want empathy or* advice?"

S/he relaxes his or her jaw, unclenches his or her fists, and exhales deeply. *"Thanks so much for just listening, empathy is just what I need. You have no idea how much stress I'm under at work."*

You say, *"No problem . It sounds like you'd appreciate having the space to talk about it. Why don't you tell me more?"*

You go from there. You listen while s/he talks and relaxes. S/he feels heard, understood, and valued.

Just listening without offering any advice might feel like a stretch; it might seem very different from the way you currently talk to each other. Good. You're reading this so you have an alternative from the way you normally communicate. This way works. It will help bring you closer to each other .

You are listening empathetically if . . .

- Your partner comes to you with a painful problem and you ask, "Do you want empathy or do you want advice?"

- You're first reaction is listening instead of offering your partner a solution.

- Instead of running away, you say to your partner, "I have some strong feelings

- about this; could you just listen and give me empathy."

- You think your partner is wrong, but you say, "I'm confused. Can you clarify what you meant?" Here is what I think I heard.

- You are willing to wait until your partner's cup is really empty before asking if s/he would like to hear any ideas or advice.

SUMMARY

Old Destructive Habits:

Fixing , Fighting and Fleeing

Fixing. You jump in and offer your advice and solutions at the first sign of an upset or problem without being asked. You try and FIX your partner. You are communicating that s/he isn't competent, and then s/he often feels judged and misunderstood.

You start to argue and make them wrong. You're angry and want your partner to do things differently.

Fighting. Of course, fighting can be very uncomfortable and you or your partner may try FLEEING as a solution,

Fleeing. It can be done by leaving the scene or by staying physically, yet checking out emotionally and mentally.

New Productive Habit: Empathetic Listening

Listen with compassion, acceptance, and understanding. Try to understand your partner's story and enter his or her world. Sometimes, it's also helpful to say what you think you heard so your partner will know if he or she is understood.

When you accept what is happening and take time to connect and understand your partner, it is a natural result for him or her to be more open.

EXERCISES

1) Watch some dramas, sitcoms, and talk shows with your partner. Notice the FATAL F's that arise. How do the characters handle uncomfortable and emotional situations? Do they fix, fight, and/or flee? Do they include more than one F? You can also consider couples whom both of you know; how do they handle these situations? Which F's do they use? How does the conversation progress? Does it go from fixing, to fighting, to fleeing? Or, do they have one strategy that they always use?

Situation: _____

Primary F: _____

Progression: _____

Result: _____

How could they change their patterns?

_____

_____

_____

_____

2) **Examine the FATAL F's that your parents' used**? Did they always follow the same conversational progression? If so, what was it? Give your responses simultaneously. Share your discoveries with you partner.

Situation: _____

Primary F: _____

Progression: _____

Result: _____

How could they change their patterns?

_____

_____

_____

_____

3) **Remember a time when you were fixing, fighting, and/or flee-ing in a situation with your partner.** Which F did you use? Did it progress to include more than one F? How did it turn out? Knowing what you know now, how would you handle it differently? Write it down and share the information?

Situation: _____

Primary F: _____

Was there a progression? _____

Result: _____

How would you do it differently now?

_____

_____

_____

_____

QUIZ: Are You a Fixer?

(Have fun and see how honest you can be!)

1. When I ask my partner to do something, I feel like I have to check to make sure it's done right.
   A. Mostly False
   B. Sometimes True
   C. Mostly True

2. My partner needs my advice to be able to make sound financial and career decisions.
   A. Mostly False
   B. Sometimes True
   C. Mostly True

3. If only my partner changed the way s/he thought, s/he could be much happier.
   A. Mostly False
   B. Sometimes True
   C. Mostly True

4. If my spouse did things my way and listened to my advice, life would be much better.
   A. Mostly False
   B. Sometimes True
   C. Mostly True

5. I am hurting the relationship if I allow my partner to remain ignorant about something. I shouldn't worry about offending him or her by offering the truth.
   A. Mostly False
   B. Sometimes True
   C. Mostly True

6. When my partner complains to me about something, I like to offer advice to help solve his or her problem.
   A. Mostly False
   B. Sometimes True
   C. Mostly True

7. If I leave my partner alone to figure something out instead of rushing to help, I will generally regret that choice later.
   A. Mostly False
   B. Sometimes True
   C. Mostly True

8. When my partner makes a big mistake, I feel frustrated, disappointed, and embarrassed. At times, I even feel like it was my fault for not preventing it from happening.
   A. Mostly False
   B. Sometimes True
   C. Mostly True

9. It is more important to me to get things done right than to worry about hurting my partner's feelings.
   A. Mostly False
   B. Sometimes True
   C. Mostly True

10. If my partner doesn't do what I say, it means I am not appreciated or respected.
    A. Mostly False
    B. Sometimes True
    C. Mostly True

Scoring:

0 points for every A

1 point for every B

2 points for every C

Your Total Score _____

If you scored between 0 and 6: You aren't a fixer at all. In fact, you're a great listener and probably have an intimate, compassionate connection with your partner.

If you scored between 7 and 13: You're a moderate fixer. You may know when to help your partner and when to hold your tongue, but sometimes, you give advice when your partner is looking for empathy.

If you scored between 14 and 20: Look Out! You're a major fixer! You may be causing yourself and your partner some distress with your constant fixing.

ADVANCED-TRAINING-VIDEO PRESENTATIONS

When your communication falls apart , so does your relationship. As a special bonus gift to you for purchasing this book, I am giving you free access to my 7-part advanced-relationship-communication series.

In the fifth video, I clear up the pieces of the communication puzzle.

Video #5
CLEARING-UP-THE-RELATIONSHIP-COMMUNICATION PUZZLE

In this video, I cover:

1. A picture that simplifies, clarifies, and greatly reduces the complexity of communication – the four pieces that increase intimacy and the four pieces that destroy it.

2. Powerful compassionate-communication tools you can use with your lover, your children, your parents, your friends – even at work! *Introduction to The 4-Step Method to Instant Intimacy.*

3. How to get what you want from your lover in a way that they enjoy giving it to you.

Go to www.MagicRelationship.net/bookbonus.htm and enter you name and email and get instant access to your free videos today.

MAKE EXTRAORDINARY COMMUNICATION A REALITY

> "What seems to us bitter trials are
> often blessings in disguise."
> – Oscar Wilde

The Four Steps for Creating Change

Now you know what *to do* and what *not to do* when communicating. The big question becomes, how do you make these changes last?

These four simple and effective steps will help you change old habits that don't serve you into new habits that do. They will guide you to freedom from Case-Building, Storytelling, Message-Assuming, Cup-Stuffing, and the Fatal F's.

1) Awareness

The first step is to become aware of what the five destructive communication habits are and how they can be running, and wrecking, your relationship.

Once you recognize these habits, you will start to see them everywhere! Be gentle on yourself and your partner during this phase. It's easy to get down on yourself. It's not that you are behaving more destructively than before, but that you are now able to recognize the behavior as destructive.

2) Understanding

Next, you'll actively start to understand the impact these habits have on your life. You'll start seeing the detrimental effects and costs to your relationship. The clearer and more real this picture is the easier change becomes.

One way you can do this is by explaining the five destructive habits to your partner. (It also works with family members and other important relationships.) and then asking for some open and honest feedback about what it's like to communicate with you. It's a bold move, but very powerful, effective, and motivating.

3) Agreement

The Key to change is "YOU GOTTA WANT IT"

Once you are aware and understand the price you are paying for keeping the old habits; it's time for you to decide if you're ready to change.

Understanding the situation doesn't mean you'll necessarily agree to change your habits. You may understand that smoking is not healthy and that it's killing you; people can tell you all of the reasons why you shouldn't smoke; the price of cigarettes can increase; and you still will not quit until you agree and commit to doing whatever it takes to stop.

If you are aware of these destructive habits, if you understand how they're screwing up your relationships, and if you AGREE that you want to change them, then you are ready for the next step.

4) Action

In this phase, you'll set yourself up to succeed. Slow down communication: empathize, listen, check out messages, and don't take things personally when possible.

Many times, we take communication with our partners very seriously because we aren't sure if we are loved or valued. Start with the assumption that you are loved and valued, and trust it, that is why you are in an intimate relationship.

Then, make it fun, make it a game, and don't take it so seriously!

Acknowledge your progress and laugh at your mistakes; enjoy learning something new. Start small. Celebrate all your successes with your partner, including the little ones.

You can even have an awards ceremony at a nice restaurant or at home with candles and music! The more fun you have, the easier, quicker, and more enjoyable your progress will be. This will support you in building a relationship based on open and honest communication that is full of trust, compassion, and intimacy.

Re-read and Review:

You're building communication and relationship muscles. Be compassionate with yourself; you're learning to use language in a whole new way. With that in mind, I recommend you re-read, review, and digest this book at least five times over the next couple of months.

Why? Because what you repeat becomes a pattern and patterns become habits. By reviewing this material, you are making sure that the habits you create are helping you build a more loving, open, and intimate relationship.

Take it to bed with you. Read it out loud to each other before going to sleep. Each time you re-read it, you will pick up new nuances about each habit.

Also, the repetition will help anchor these habits into your memory so you fully understand them and are aware of them.

Commitment:

Once you agree that you want to change things, take action! Remember to work with small doable daily steps. This book is full of small exercises that you can implement once you commit to change. Here are some more examples:

- Need a gentle reminder? Get a rubber band and put it on your left wrist. Every time you become aware that you're falling into one of your old habits, pull the rubber band and let it snap. It's a little reminder that increases your awareness and motivation to change the behavior.

- Every time you fall into an old destructive habit, write it down. Sometimes, you will realize it right after it happens. Other times, it will take hours, days, or weeks, for you to see that your behavior is falling into an old pattern. Record it whenever you become aware of it, and then be vulnerable and share the list with your partner.

It will feel awkward and uncomfortable at first. I play racket-ball and I'm right-handed, so every once in a while, for a challenge, I will play left-handed.

I want to tell you upfront that any time you make a commitment to changing your life, you will be tested.

For example, many years ago, I decided to quit smoking. I told one of my closest buddies that I was trying to break this tough and nasty habit. I hoped for some words of encouragement and support, but instead, he offered to give me a free carton of cigarettes.

I was pretty angry with him at the time. But as I look back on it now, I can see that my intentions for leading a healthier life and changing my habit were being tested.

You will be tested and tempted to go back to the old communication habits. You may find yourself building cases, getting stuck in damaging stories, Message-Assuming without taking the time to clarify, trying to stuff already full cups, and of course, fixing, fighting, and fleeing.

As you practice what you have discovered and stay committed to changing your communication habits, things will start to change!

Make This Commitment To:

- yourself

- your partner

- your future

- being open, honest, and compassionate

- developing your relationship skills

- creating a great, satisfying, and fun relationship.

- Once you commit and start practicing your new skills, you may be pleasantly surprised by your results.

Some of the benefits you and your partner can expect:

- spending less time in reaction and more time in open and honest communication with each other

- Being more trustong, honest, and open in your communications with each other

- Being more appreciative, affectionate, and respectful to each other

- you both look forward to sitting down and talking openly and honestly

- feeling heard, understood, and valued on a more regular basis.

- having less aggressive and less defensive communication

- not taking things personally or making things personal

- you're able to have productive disagreements and conversations without spiraling

- downward into painful arguments, blaming, and make-wrong game.

- being able to have productive disagreements and conversations without spiraling downward into painful arguments, blaming, and making each other wrong.

- spending less time dealing with drama, trauma, and stress, and have more time for passion, romance, and intimacy!

ADVANCED-TRAINING-VIDEO PRESENTATIONS

Discover the biggest hidden enemy to your relationship… it's not what you think. I will cover this in the 6th video on relationship communication.

Video #6
THE BIGGEST ENEMY TO A GREAT RELATIONSHIP

In this video, I cover:

1. The secret key to having a healthy relationship – how you can use this with your lover, and with your kids.

2. What an EKG machine can show you about the likelihood of your relationship succeeding. Can being too comfortable wreck your relationship?

3. What playing left-handed racquetball can teach you about how to grow your relationship.

Go to www.MagicRelationship.net/bookbonus.htm, enter you name and email address to get instant access to your free videos today.

BOOK SUMMARY

THE 5 DESTRUCTIVE HABITS THAT DESTROY A LOVING RELATIONSHIP

> **"With the gift of listening comes the gift of healing."**
> **– Catherine de Hueck Doherty**

Here is a quick review of the 5 habits.

PRINT THESE PAGES OUT or DOWNLOAD THE PDF.

(www.MagicRelationship.net/summary.pdf)

Make sure to put it where you will see it daily. Tape them to your fridge, hang them on your bulletin board, and post them in your bedroom.

Destructive Habit 1: Case-Building

You gather evidence to use against your partner, including guilt, blame, and shame, to argue your case. You want to be understood but you don't care about understanding your partner. Building a case leaves your partner alienated and feeling bad, stupid, and wrong.

New Habit 1: Connection-Building

You choose to build a connection from understanding, compassion, acceptance, and support. When you do this, you fill your relationship with trust, intimacy, openness, and honest communication.

Tip: Before talking, ask yourself, "Do I want to build a case against my partner or a connection with him or her?"

Rule: Avoid judgmental words like should/shouldn't, right/wrong, or good/bad.

Action: Ask questions to understand your partner's point of view rather than gathering evidence to prove you're right. Listen and empathize. When in doubt, say, ***"Please tell me more . . . "***

Destructive Habit 2: Storytelling

You get stuck in destructive and defensive stories. **The unexamined story is experienced as reality.** You become convinced that your story is true without discussing it with your partner

New Habit 2: Story-Busting

The mind is a meaning-making machine. Check to see if the meanings are accurate. Story busting helps you break free from old stories that don't help you or your relationship. Meet your partner with openness and curiosity.

Tip: Remember, just because you feel certain, it doesn't mean you are right.

Rule: Check out your story before acting on it. Go for the truth beyond your stories.

Action: If there is an upset or misunderstanding start by saying, *"I'm telling myself the story that . . ."* end with, *"Is that true?"*

Destructive Habit 3: Message-Assuming

The **message sent is rarely the message received.** Assuming you know what your partner meant to say leads to confusion, misunderstandings, and upsets. Assuming that you were heard and understood is also dangerous.

New Habit 3: Message-Clarifying

Check in on a regular basis during important conversations. Make sure that what the other person understands is what you are trying to communicate. If you are listening, make sure to repeat back what you think you heard your partner say.

Tip: If the conversation is important and emotional, *go slow, speak in small chunks,* and frequently repeat back what you think you heard your partner say.

Rule: Whether you're talking or listening, don't let more than forty words be said without checking in.

Action: When you are speaking, ask, *"Can you tell me what you heard me say?"* When you are listening, ask, *"Can I tell you what I think I heard you say?"*

Destructive Habit 4: Cup-Stuffing

When your partner is full of emotion and dealing with problems, or just hyper-focused, they can't hear you. If you demand their attention when their cup is already full, you rarely get what you want. Instead, you get explosions, meltdowns, and withdrawal.

New Habit 4: Cup-Emptying

Listen first, and then offer empathy: it will help empty your partner's cup. Also, take the time to empty your own cup.

Tip: Agree that if someone says, 'Cup full", you either help empty their full cup or give them space. Remember, it's not personal.

Rule: If you say, "Cup full', be responsible for reconnecting with your partner later.

Action: When your partner says "Cup Full", ask him or her, *"Do you need empathy or do you need space?"*

Destructive Habit 5: The Fatal F's

Fixing, Fighting, and Fleeing: Offering solutions to your partner's problems is called "**Fixing.**" People often become defensive when receiving unasked for advice. This can lead to "**Fighting**." When that doesn't work, one or both of you checks out emotionally, physically, or verbally, which is what we call "Fleeing."

New Habit 5. **Listening Empathetically Always.**

Offer empathy first! It's the best place to start and will help you understand what your partner is feelings before you offer any advice.

Tip: Only give advice when it is asked for.

Rule: If you're upset, be sure to ask for empathy, space, and whatever else you need.

Action: Ask, *"Do you want empathy or advice?"*

ADVANCED-TRAINING-VIDEO PRESENTATIONS

In this video, I cover:

Video #7
THE GREATEST GIFT YOU CAN GIVE…
IT'S NOT WHAT YOU THINK!

I saved the most fun for last. In the seventh video, we will explore 'The Greatest Gift You Can Give.' The answer will surprise and may even, shock you with its' simplicity and accuracy.

1. Are you treating your relationship like a business and making this common mistake? Discover what it is and how to turn it around.

2. This one tip is worth watching the whole video series to master. A simple and powerful question that will stop many conflicts right in their tracks and almost instantly bring back the loving connection you desire.

3. A short exercise you can do to instantly make your lover feel appreciated and acknowledged.

Watch these 7 videos with your lover and increase the amount love and intimacy you both feel in your relationship.

Go to www.MagicRelationship.net/bookbonus.htm, enter you name and email address, and get instant access to your free videos today.

For more information on upcoming workshops, seminars, and other materials help you bring more love, intimacy, and understanding to your relationship, to www.MagicRelationship.com.

you are interested in private and personalized relationship coaching, give my fice a call, and we can set up an appointment to see how I can help.

ABOUT THE AUTHOR

> "Every interaction is a chance to change the world"
> - Kathleen Sacht

After spending nearly 20 years as a commercial fisherman in Alaska, Paul Sterling made a major career change due to some deeply painful and confusing personal events in his life.

On a quest to understand why people do what they do, he traveled around the world to study communication skills and human behavior with the some of the top leaders in the field: Marshall Rosenberg (creator of "Nonviolent Communication"), Richard Bandler (co-developer of NLP: Neuro-Linguistic Programming), Robert Kiyosaki (author of *Rich Dad, Poor Dad*), Bob Proctor (motivational speaker and contributor to "The Secret"), Marshall Thurber (creator of "Money & You" cc and "Powerful Presentations"), and Tony Robbins (author of "Unlimited Power").

Based on his training in the dynamics of human behavior and communication skills, Mr. Sterling developed a method of enhancing efficiency and productivity for businesses and organizations. This method uses leadership skills, quality control, systems thinking, and management communication tools.

Almost 20 years ago, his mission shifted from business consulting to focusing on compassionate communication for improving and empowering couples' relationships.

Blending his background in Systems Theory and Neuro-Linguistic Programming with the principles of "Nonviolent Communication", Paul created a powerful, simple, and useful system for transforming the way couples communicate in their relationships.

It's called **The Magic Relationship Method**

Mr. Sterling has been asked to share his **Magic Relationship Method** with a wide variety of organizations, including Naropa University (staff & professors), Estes Park Restorative Justice Organization, and Goodwill Industries of Denver.

The Denver School District brought him in to work with their at-risk high-school students, and he also taught communication skills to prison inmates at Jeffco Jail for 8 years with great success. His greatest passion is teaching compassionate communication skills to couples.

Paul Sterling currently lives in Estes Park, Colorado. He travels around the country, and occasionally abroad, teaching transformational communication to couples, individuals, and organizations. When the local rivers are thawed, he enjoys kayaking and fly-fishing.

Made in the USA
Middletown, DE
12 January 2017